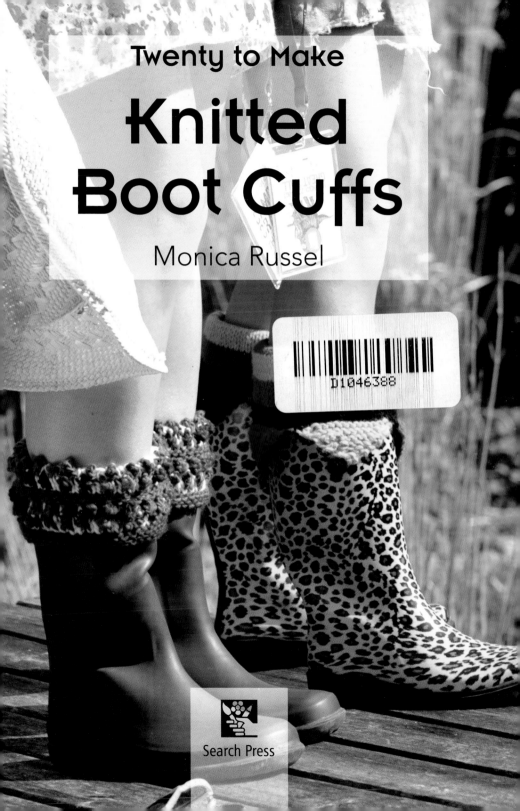

Twenty to Make
Knitted Boot Cuffs

Monica Russel

Search Press

First published in Great Britain 2012

Search Press Limited
Wellwood, North Farm Road,
Tunbridge Wells, Kent TN2 3DR

Text copyright © Monica Russel 2012

Photographs by Debbie Patterson on location

Photographs and design copyright
© Search Press Ltd 2012

ISBN: 978-1-84448-849-0

Suppliers
If you have difficulty in obtaining any of the
materials and equipment mentioned in this book,
then please visit the Search Press website for
details of suppliers: www.searchpress.com

Printed in Malaysia

Dedication

*To Trevor, Matthew, Jacob and
Claerwen for their encouragement, ideas
and support; and to Jeannine for her
willingness to act as my sample model.*

Abbreviations

beg: beginning

DPN: double-pointed needles

inc: increase (by working into the front and
back of the stitch)

k: knit

k2tog: knit two stitches together

knitwise: as though to knit

p: purl

p2tog: purl two stitches together

PM: place marker

psso: pass slipped stitch over

rem: remaining

rep: repeat

sl: slip, usually slip 1 stitch

st(s): stitch(es)

tbl: through back loop

WS: wrong side

*: repeat the instructions following the * as
many times as specified

Contents

Introduction 4

Knitting know-how 6

Bramble 8

Imperium 10

Art Deco Autumn 12

Boots in Bloom 14

Hemingway 16

Clarice 18

March of the Penguins 20

Allure 22

Love My Boot Cuff 24

Rasta Jester 26

Oakshield 28

Blueberry Bouclé 30

Electric Kicks 32

Puss-in-Boots 34

Pig in the Grass 36

Sunrise 38

Parisienne 40

Fair Isle 42

Quackers 44

Hearthlight 46

Introduction

This book brings together a wide range of knitted cuffs, toppers, hugs and covers for all types of boots, be they fashion, wellington or walking boots. Smart and practical, these cuffs bring a touch of colour, style and individuality to everyday wear as well as keeping your legs warm and draught-free.

The patterns in this book can make your favourite pair of boots even more versatile, and they also give you, the knitter, the chance to try something new, challenging and unusual. The patterns offer opportunities for knitters of all abilities, from novice knitters to the more experienced. The eclectic range of designs covers fun, simple motifs like pigs and penguins, and a wide variety of more sophisticated textures including cables, bobbles and lace. Some of the bolder designs were inspired by the strong lines and vibrant colours of Art Deco, a personal favourite style of mine.

This book has been fun and challenging to write, and has given me the incentive to indulge myself in bright colours, subtle shades and luxurious yarns. I have really enjoyed having the time to be creative and develop my own ideas.

These boot cuffs cater for all age and tastes, and colours can always be substituted for those given. The ideas for the patterns can be transferred to other accessories to enhance and co-ordinate anyone's wardrobe. I hope you enjoy knitting them all!

Opposite

Whether you call them hugs, toppers or cuffs, these fantastic accessories are functional, attractive and fun. They can revitalise a favourite pair of boots; enhancing a classic style or giving a fresh new look. Perhaps best of all, they add comfort and warmth to your boots, so even your festival wellies can be comfortable and stylish!

Knitting know-how

General notes

The sizes of the boot cuffs given in the projects are for an average-sized boot. The patterns can be adapted: try making them bigger for wellington boots or smaller for short fashion boots.

Yarn and tensions

All the boot cuffs in this book have been knitted in natural fibres. I chose to knit in Artesano and Manos Del Uruguay yarns for their luxurious feel and quality, but any comparable weight yarn will work. All tensions given are for stocking stitch.

Super Chunky yarn:

Artesano Super Chunky (Super Bulky) 50% superfine alpaca/50% Peruvian highland wool

Tension: 7.5 sts in 9 rows in 10cm (4in) using 12mm (UK -; US 17) needles.

Yardage: 100g; 33m (36yd).

Aran weight yarn:

Artesano Aran 50% alpaca/50% Peruvian highland wool.

Tension: 17sts in 21 rows using 5mm (UK 6; US 8) needles

Yardage: 100g; 132m (144yd).

DK pure alpaca yarn:

Artesano DK 100% pure superfine alpaca.

Tension: 22sts and 30 rows using 4mm (UK 8; US 6) needles.

Yardage: 50g; 100m (109yd).

Textured aran yarn:

Manos Del Uruguay Wool Clasica handspun kettle-dyed 100% pure wool.

Tension: 14–18sts in 10cm (4in) row.

Yardage: approx. 100g; 125m (138yd).

> **Knitting note**
> Use the DK pure alpaca yarn double throughout the patterns.

> **Knitting note**
> Twist the textured aran yarn every three to four sts to avoid long loops at the back of your work.

Needles

For these projects I used both straight and double-pointed needles made from sustainable wood. I find these great to knit with because of their durability, and they are flexible enough to work with in all temperatures. The double-pointed needles were only used to cast on with before transferring to circular needles.

I used 60cm (23½in) circular needles for the thicker boot cuffs but these could equally well be knitted using straight needles.

All single-pointed needles come in pairs and double-pointed needles come in sets of five.

Bramble

Materials:

Three 100g hanks of Super Chunky (Super Bulky) yarn – purple

1 stitch marker

Needles:

1 set of 7mm (UK 2; US 10½) double-pointed knitting needles, 19cm (7.5in)

1 10mm (UK 000; US 15) circular needle, 60cm (23½in)

Large-eyed tapestry needle

Instructions:

Cuffs

Make two.

Using 7mm DPN and purple yarn, cast on 29 sts, distributing the stitches evenly across four of the needles.

Do not turn work. Join this first round by slipping the first cast-on stitch on to the left-hand needle. PM on right-hand needle (this is to mark the beginning of the round), and knit this slipped stitch together with the last cast-on stitch. You will now have 28sts (7 on each of the DPNs).

Rows 1–16: *k1, p 1* rep to the end of the row. These 16 rows form the cuff of the piece. Be careful to move your stitch marker at the end of each row.

Legs

Continuing from the cuffs, change to the 10mm (UK 000; US 15) circular needle and begin bramble stitch as follows. The pattern repeat is over four stitches. Remember to PM after each completed round.

Round 1: p.

Round 2: *p1, k1, p1* all into next st, k3 together, rep set pattern to the end of the round.

Round 3: p.

Round 4: k3tog, *p1, k1, p1*, rep set pattern to the end of the round.

These four rounds create the bramble stitch. Rep the four rounds one more time and then rep row 1 once more. Cast off sts purlwise.

Making up

Using a large-eyed tapestry needle, sew in all of the ends.

These boot cuffs will give a different look to a favourite pair of boots. Try knitting them in cream yarn for a classic monochrome look.

Imperium

Materials:

Three 100g hanks of Super Chunky (Super Bulky) yarn – blue

1 stitch marker

Needles:

1 10mm (UK 000; US 15) circular needle, 60cm (23½in)

Large-eyed tapestry needle

Instructions:

Make two.

Using 10mm circular needles cast on 33sts loosly in blue. Place marker on right needle (this is to mark the beginning of the round).

Slip the first cast-on stitch to the left-hand needle, then knit this slipped stitch together with the last cast-on stitch. You will now have 32sts on your needle.

Remember to move the marker at the end of each round.

Rows 1–24: *k1, p1* rep to the end of the row. Cast off sts loosly following rib pattern.

Making up

Using a large-eyed tapestry needle, sew in all of the ends.

A great simple pattern makes these cuffs perfect to keep feet snug while you are hard at work in the garden. Try making them in green to make a handsome complement to traditional wellies.

Art Deco Autumn

Materials:

100g hanks of textured aran yarn – mustard (A) and green (B)

Small amount of textured aran yarn – brown (C)

Needles:

1 pair of 5mm (UK 6; US 8) single-pointed knitting needles

1 pair of 6mm (UK 4; US 10) single-pointed knitting needles

Large-eyed tapestry needle

Instructions:

Make two.

Using 5mm (UK 6; US 8) needles, cast on 54sts in mustard yarn.

Row 1: *k2, p2* rep to last 2 sts, k2.

Row 2: *p2, k2* rep to last 2 sts, p2.

Rows 19–21: Rep the last 2 rows nine more times and then row 1 once more.

Row 22: p1, inc 1 into next st, continue in rib until 54th st, inc 1, p last sts. You will now have 56 sts on your needle.

Change to 6mm needles and work 14 rows from the chart.

Work the pattern from stitch 1–26, then rep the whole chart once more.

Work sts 3–6 once more (this ensures you do not end up with a thick green seam).

Cut off yarns A and C.

Rib rows 1 and 2: *k2, p2* rep to end. Cast off.

Making up

Sew in loose ends by weaving them into sts at the back of your work.

With right side facing, use a mattress stitch to join the side seams of the pattern component of the boot cuff.

Sew up the rib on the rear side of the boot cuff.

Knitting note

Cut yarn C into small lengths to make working with three colours more manageable.

A	B	C

	26	25	24	23	22	21	20	19	18	17	16	15	14	13	12	11	10	9	8	7	6	5	4	3	2	1	
14																											14
13																											13
12																											12
11																											11
10																											10
9																											9
8																											8
7																											7
6																											6
5																											5
4																											4
3																											3
2																											2
1																											1
	26	25	24	23	22	21	20	19	18	17	16	15	14	13	12	11	10	9	8	7	6	5	4	3	2	1	

The pattern for these elegant boot cuffs is suitable for an experienced knitter. The autumnal colours complement long brown boots very well.

Boots in Bloom

Materials:

100g hanks of textured aran
yarn – lilac (colour A) and
cerise (colour B)

Small amounts of textured aran
yarn – light pink (colour C)
and mid blue (colour D)

Needles:

1 pair of 5mm (UK 6; US 8) single-
pointed knitting needles

1 pair of 6mm (UK 4; US 10) single-
pointed knitting needles

Large-eyed tapestry needle

Instructions:

Make two.

Using 5mm (UK 6; US 8) needles,
cast on 52sts with yarn A.

Rows 1–18: *k2, p2* rep to the
end of row. Cut off yarn A.

Rows 19–20: Change to 6mm
needles. Using colour B,
k to end.

Note: Yarn B will now be the
main colour for the rest of the
boot cuff.

Patterned section

Start working from the chart
as follows:

Row 1: k6 colour B, place first
flower using colour C; k8 colour
B, place second flower in colour
D; k8 colour B, place third
flower in colour A, k6.

Centre of flowers:

1st flower: blue (colour D)

2nd flower: lilac (colour A)

3rd flower: light pink (colour C)

Continue working from rows
2–11 of the chart.

Row 12: purl

Row 13: knit

Row 14: *k1, inc 1 (into the
same stitch)* rep to the end of
row. Cast off.

Making up

Sew in loose ends by weaving
them into stitches at the back
of your work. With the right
side facing, use a mattress
stitch to join the side seams of
the pattern component of the
boot cuff.

Sew up the rib on the rear
side of the boot cuff.

Knitting note

After the rib, cut yarns C,
A and D into lengths of
approximately 2m (78¾in)
to make the intarsia flowers
more manageable.

	13	12	11	10	9	8	7	6	5	4	3	2	1		
11															11
10															10
9															9
8															8
7															7
6															6
5															5
4															4
3															3
2															2
1															1
	13	12	11	10	9	8	7	6	5	4	3	2	1		

A B D

These cheerful cuffs will add a new lease of life and originality to your boots, whatever the length.

Hemingway

Materials:

2 x 100g hanks of textured aran yarn –
cream (women's) or variegated (men's)

Needles:

1 pair of 5mm (UK 6; US 8) single-pointed knitting needles

1 pair of 6mm (UK 4; US 10) single-pointed
knitting needles

Large-eyed tapestry needle

Cable needle

Instructions:

Women's

Make two.

Using 5mm (UK 6; US 8)
needles, cast on 52sts in
cream yarn.

Rows 1–21: work rows in k2/
p2 rib.

Row 22: Using set rib pattern,
increase on second and every
following twelfth st. [56sts]

Men's

Make two.

Using 5mm (UK 6; US 8)
needles, cast on 60sts in
variegated yarn.

Rows 1–25: work rows in k2/
p2 rib.

Row 26: Inc 1 on every fifth
st. [72sts]

Change to 6mm (UK 4; US 10)
needles and insert knotted
cable as follows:

Knotted cable section

This is worked over 6 sts on a
background of reverse st st.

Cable block: (RS) k2, p2, k2

Rows 1, 5, 7 and 9 (women's):
p3, *insert cable block, p3*
rep from * to * until last 8sts,
insert cable block, p2.

Rows 1, 5, 7 and 9 (men's):
p2, *insert cable block, p3*
rep from * to * until last 7sts,
insert cable block, p1.

Row 2 (women's : k2 *insert
cable block, k3* rep from * to
* to the end of the row.

Row 2 (men's): k1 *insert
cable block, k3* rep from *
to * to last 8 st, insert cable
block, k2.

Row 3: p3, *cable 6 – slip next
4 sts on to cable needle and
hold at front of work, knit next
2 sts from left-hand needle,
then slip the 2 purl sts from
the cable needle back to the
left-hand needle. Pass the
cable needle with 2 remaining
knit sts to the back of work,
purl sts from left-hand needle,
then knit the sts from the
cable needle; p3* rep until
last 8sts, repeat cable block
once more, p2.

Making a bobble

MB: To make bobble, (k1, yo,
k1, yo, k1) into next stitch,
turn and p5, turn and k1, sl1,
k2tog, psso, k1, turn and
p3tog.

With right side facing, knit
into the bobble stitch again.

Spacing the bobble row

Next row (women's): p1, MB,
p1 *insert cable block, p1,
MB, p1*, rep from * to * until
last 8sts, insert cable block,
MB, p1.

Next row (men's): p2 *insert
cable block, p1, MB, p1*,
rep from * to * until last 7sts,
insert cable block, p1.

Remember to knit into the
bobble stitch again before
continuing with the pattern

Next row: As row 2.

Next 4 rows: *k2, p2* rep to
end. Cast off.

Making up

Using a large-eyed tapestry
needle, sew in all of the ends.

With right side facing, use
a mattress stitch to join the
side seams of the pattern
component of the boot cuff.

Sew up the rib on the rear
side of the boot cuff.

Two hanks of variegated aran yarn were used for this version of the boot cuffs. Even a simple change in colour can alter the character of your projects, so have fun experimenting.

Clarice

Materials:

100g hanks of aran yarn – bright green (A), black (B), orange (C), and light cream (D)

Needles:

1 pair of 5mm (UK 6; US 8) single-pointed knitting needles

Large-eyed tapestry needle

Instructions:

Make two.

Using 5mm (UK 6; US 8)needles, cast on 54sts in A.

Row 1: *K3, P3* repeat to end.

Rows 2–22: as above.

Pattern section

Use the chart, repeat sts 1–27 once to match your 54sts on the needle. See note on chart for chequered repeat.

Row 17: Knit

Row 18: Cast off sts.

Knitting note

The two chequered borders continue with B and C in sequence across the row. All other lines do a complete pattern repeat from stitch 1.

Making up

Using a large-eyed tapestry needle, sew in all of the loose ends by weaving them into stitches at the back of your work.

With right side facing, use a mattress stitch to join the side seams of the pattern component of the boot cuff.

Sew up the rib on the rear side of the boot cuff.

C	A	B	D

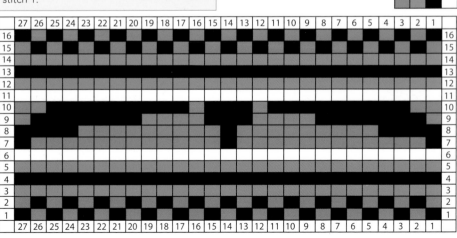

	27	26	25	24	23	22	21	20	19	18	17	16	15	14	13	12	11	10	9	8	7	6	5	4	3	2	1	
16																												16
15																												15
14																												14
13																												13
12																												12
11																												11
10																												10
9																												9
8																												8
7																												7
6																												6
5																												5
4																												4
3																												3
2																												2
1																												1
	27	26	25	24	23	22	21	20	19	18	17	16	15	14	13	12	11	10	9	8	7	6	5	4	3	2	1	

This design was inspired by my great love for Art Deco design. The bright colours will cheer you up on a winter's day.

March of the Penguins

Materials:

2 x 50g hanks of DK pure alpaca yarn – pale turquoise (A)

50g hanks of DK pure alpaca yarn – gold (B), mid-blue (C) and cream (D)

Needles:

1 pair of 5mm (UK 6; US 8) single-pointed knitting needles

Large-eyed tapestry needle

Instructions:

Make two.

Cast on 58sts in yarn A.

Knit into the back of the sts to form a neat edge.

Using the chart place pattern as follows:

Even row numbers are knit and odd numbers are purl.

Row 1: k2A, *3B, 2A, 3B, 6A* rep from * to * three times more.

Continue working from the chart until row 18. Cut off yarn

C. The rest of the knitting is done in yarn A.

Row 19: knit.

Row 20: purl.

Now continue in ribbing.

Ribbing

Row 1: *k2, p2* rep until the last two sts, k2.

Row 2: *p2, k2* rep until the last two sts, p2.

Rows 3–20: Rep rows 1 and 2 nine more times.

Row 21: As row 1.

Row 22: Cast off sts.

Making up

Use the tapestry needle to sew in loose ends by weaving them into stitches at the back of your work.

With right side facing, use a mattress stitch to join the side seams of the pattern component of the boot cuff.

Sew up the rib on the rear side of the boot cuff.

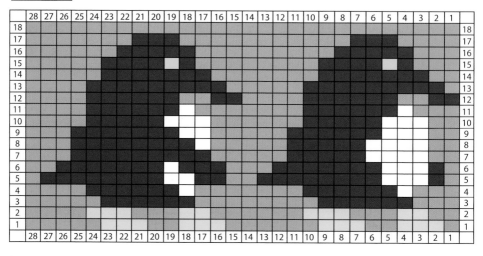

Penguins are always fun to work with and these cuffs will liven up any boots. This pattern is suitable for a knitter who has mastered the basics. To change the look, try knitting them in different colours.

Allure

Materials:

100g hanks of aran yarn – black (A)
and white (B)

Needles:

1 pair of 5mm (UK 6; US 8) single-pointed knitting needles
1 pair of 5.5mm (UK 5; US 9) single-pointed knitting needles
Large-eyed tapestry needle

Instructions:

Make two.

Using 5mm (UK 5; US 8) needles cast on 54sts
in yarn A.

Row 1: *k2, p2* rep to last 2 sts, k2.

Row 2: *p2, k2* rep to last 2 sts p2.

Rows 3–22: Rep rows 1 and 2 ten more times.

Pattern

To set the pattern: Purl in yarn A decreasing 1
stitch on 26th stitch (53sts on needle).

Row 1: (Right side) Using yarn B, (k1, sl 1) 5
times; * k12, sl 1, (k1, sl1) four times * rep * to *
once more to last st, k1.

Row 2: Using colour B, (p1, sl1) five times, *p12,
sl1 (p1, sl1) four times; rep * to * once more to
last st, p1.

Row 3: Using colour A, k2, sl 1, (k1, sl1) three
times; * k14, sl 1, (k1, sl1) three times*; Rep * to
* once more to last 2 sts, k2.

Row 4: Using colour A, p2, sl 1, (p1, sl1), three
times; *p14, sl 1, (p1, sl1) three times* repeat *
to * once more to last 2 sts, p2

Row 5–20: Rep rows 1–4 four more times.

Rows 21–22: Rep rows 1 and 2 once more. Cut
off yarn B.

Cast off sts using yarn A.

Making up

Sew in loose ends by weaving them into the
stitches at the back of your work.

With right side facing, use a mattress stitch to
join the side seams of the pattern component
of the boot cuff.

Sew up the rib on the rear side of the boot cuff.

These boot cuffs will add style to any boot. This pattern is suitable for a knitter with some experience. For a change, try knitting the cuff in colours that complement your favourite coat.

Love My Boot Cuff

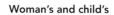

Materials:

Child's size:

2 x 50g hanks of DK pure alpaca yarn – Chile red (A)

100g hanks of textured aran yarn – black (A) and white (B)

Woman's size:

50g hank of DK pure alpaca yarn – Chile red (C)

100g hank of textured aran yarn – dark green (D)

Needles:

1 pair of 5mm (UK 6; US 8) single-pointed knitting needles

Large-eyed tapestry needle

Instructions:

Make two.

Child's

Using 5mm (UK 6; US 8) needles, cast on 48sts in A.

Rows 1–18: *k2, p2*, rep to the end of row.

Work the patterned section.

> #### Woman's
>
> Using 5mm (UK 6; US 8) needles, cast on 60sts in C.
>
> Rows 1–22: *k2, p2*, rep to the end of row.
>
> Work the patterned section.

Child's

Continue knitting in colour A.

Rows 1–4: stocking stitch starting with a knit row.

> #### Woman's
>
> Continue knitting in colour A.
>
> Rows 1–6: stocking stitch starting with a knit row.

Woman's and child's

Using the chart, insert the heart motif. Note that you will be working from the top down so the heart is in the correct position once the boot cuff is on the leg.

Row 1: k3A *k2B, k2A, k2B, k6A*; rep to last 9sts, k2A, k2B, k2A, k3A.

Rows 2–8: Follow the chart for these rows, ending with a purl row.

Rows 9–10: Work st st.

Row 13: k1A, k1B, k10A, *k1B, k11A* rep to end.

Row 14: p10A, *p3B, p9A*, rep to last 13sts, p3B p8A p3B.

> #### Woman's
>
> Row 14: p10A *p3B, p9A* rep to last 13sts, p3B, p8A, p3B, p9A, p3B.

Row 15: As row 13, cut off yarn B.

Rows 16–18: Work st st in colour A, starting with a purl row.

Row 19: Cast off.

Making up

Sew in loose ends by weaving them into stitches at the back of your work.

With right side facing, use a mattress stitch to join side seams of the pattern component of the boot cuff.

Sew up rib on the rear side of the boot cuff.

	8	7	6	5	4	3	2	1	
8		■				■	■		8
7	■	■	■	■	■	■	■	■	7
6	■	■	■	■	■	■	■	■	6
5	■	■	■	■	■	■	■	■	5
4	■	■	■	■	■	■	■	■	4
3		■	■	■	■	■	■		3
2			■	■	■	■			2
1				■	■				1
	8	7	6	5	4	3	2	1	

These adorable boot cuffs are sure to warm your heart. The smaller pair will fit a child's boots and the larger pair a woman's wellies or wide, long boots. Sizes and colours can be adjusted to suit your boot.

Rasta Jester

Materials:

2 x 50g hanks of DK pure alpaca yarn – Chile red (A)

50g hanks of DK pure alpaca yarn – gold (B), green (C), black (D)

Needles:

1 pair of 5mm (UK 6; US 8) single-pointed knitting needles

Large-eyed tapestry needle

Instructions:

Make two.

Using colour A, cast on 1 st.
Row 1: knit.

Using cable cast on, cast on 1st on each side of every alternate row (odd row numbers) until you have 15sts on your needle. Knit every even row.

Cut off yarn after 14th row. Continue to make three more triangles in the same way, using colours B, C and D. Leave all of your triangles on one needle.

Main body

Using yarn D with wrong side facing, purl across all 4 triangles increasing 1st in between each triangle and one more increase at the end [64sts].

Next four rows: work st st stitch. Change to yarn C.

Next six rows: work st st stitch. Change to yarn B.

Next six rows: work st st stitch. Change to yarn A.

Next six rows: work st st stitch.

Ribbed top

Rows 1–19: Using yarn A, *k2, p2* rep to the end of row.

Cast off sts.

Making up

Sew in loose ends by weaving them into stitches at the back of your work.

With right side facing, use a mattress stitch to join the side seams of the pattern component of the boot cuff. Sew up the rib on the rear side of the boot cuff.

Make one bobble in each colour yarn.

Making a bobble

MB: To make bobble (k1, yo, k1, yo, k1) into next stitch, turn and p5, turn and k1, sl1, k2tog, psso, k1, turn and p3tog.

Cut off yarn and thread it through st rem on needle.

Sew end into bobble to make it rounded.

Sew bobbles on to points at the bottom of your boot cuff as follows:

Colour A bobble onto colour C point; colour B bobble onto colour D point; colour C bobble onto colour A point and colour D bobble onto colour B point.

The pointed bobbled edges add a festival feel to these boot cuffs, and they will fit wellies with ease preventing them from chafing bare summer legs. This pattern is suitable for a knitter with some experience.

Oakshield

Materials:

3 x 100g hanks of Super
    Chunky yarn – grey (A)
2 x 100g hanks of Super
    Chunky yarn – turquoise (B)

Needles:

1 10mm (UK 000; US 15) circular
    needle, 60cm (23½in)
Large-eyed tapestry needle

Instructions:

Make two.

Using the 10mm (UK 000; US 15) circular needle
and colour A, cast on 33sts loosly. PM on
right needle (this is to mark the beginning of
the round), Slip the first cast-on stitch to the
left hand needle, then knit this slipped stitch
together with the last cast-on stitch. You will
now have 32sts on your needle. Remember to
move marker at the end of each round.

Rows 1–12: *k1, p1* rep to the end of the row.

Cast off sts loosly, following rib pattern.

Rows 13–15: Change to B, knit.

Rows 16–18: Change to A, knit.

Rows 19–21: Change to B, knit.

Rows 22–23: Change to A, knit.

Cast off.

Making up

Using a large-eyed tapestry needle,
sew in all ends.

These boot cuffs will fit snugly into the top of a welly aiding warmth and comfort. The pattern can easily be adapted for a man's welliess by casting on 37sts (rather than 33sts) and decreasing to 36sts (rather than 32sts). This pattern is suitable for a knitter who has mastered the basics.

Blueberry Bouclé

Materials:

100g hanks of textured aran yarn –
cream (A), teal (B), raspberry (C)

Needles:

1 pair of 5mm (UK 6;
US 8) single-pointed
knitting needles

1 pair of 6mm (UK 4;
US 10) single-pointed
knitting needles

Large-eyed tapestry needle

Instructions:

Make two.

Using 5mm (UK 6; US 8)
needles cast on 53 sts in yarn A.

Rib

Row 1: *k2, p2* rep to last st, k1.

Row 2: p1, *k2, p2* rep to end

Rows 3–12: Rep rows 1 and 2.

Main body

Change to 6mm (UK 4; US 10) needles.

Row 1: k1 in yarn A. *Work 1 bobble in yarn B
as follows: with B, k1, y/o, pass k st over y/o
and return remaining y/o st to left needle, rep
twice more, leaving last y/o st on right needle,
k1 in yarn A*. Repeat from * to * until end of
row. Cut off yarn B.

Row 2: Using yarn A, purl.

Row 3: Using yarn C, work 1 bobble as above
k1 in yarn A, work 1 bobble using colour C.
Rep from * to * until end of row. Cut off yarn C.

Row 4: Using yarn A purl.

Rows 5–8: Rejoin yarn B, knit every row
(garter st).

Row 9: As row 3.

Row 10: As row 4.

Row 11: As row 1.

Row 12: As row 2.

Rows 13–16: Rejoin yarn C, knit every row. Cast
off sts.

Making up

Sew in loose ends by weaving them into
stitches at the back of your work.

With right side facing, use a mattress stitch to
join the side seams of the pattern component
of the boot cuff. Sew up the rib on the rear side
of the boot cuff.

The elongated bobbles give the yarn a bouclé effect and add character to the cuffs.

Electric Kicks

Materials:

2 x 50g hanks of DK alpaca
   yarn – deep turquoise (A)

1 x 50g hanks of DK alpaca
   yarn – light blue (B)

Needles:

1 pair of 5mm (UK 6; US 8) single-pointed knitting needles

Large-eyed tapestry needle

Instructions:

Make two.

Using 5mm (UK 6; US 8) needles cast on 44 sts in yarn A. Knit into the back of the sts to form a neat edge.

Rows 1–20 *k2, p2* rep to end of row.

Pattern rows

Row 21: Using yarn A (RS), knit, increasing 1st on 22nd st (45).

Row 22: Change to yarn B, purl to end.

Row 23: Using yarn B, k1 (k1, yo, k1) into next st: *sl1, (k1, yo, k1) into next st* rep from * to * to last st, k1.

Row 24: Using yarn B k1, k3tog tbl, *sl1, k3tog tbl*, rep from * to * to last st, k1.

Row 25: Change to A, knit to end.

Row 26: Using yarn A, purl to end.

Row 27: Change to yarn B, k2, (k1, yo, k1) into next st, *sl1, (k1, yo, k1) into next st: rep from * to * to last 2 sts, k2.

Row 28: Using yarn B, p2, k3tog tbl, *sl1, k3tog tbl*, rep from * to * to last 2 sts, p2.

Rows 28–43: Rep last 8 rows twice more.

Rows 44–49: Rep rows 1–6 once more.

Picot edge cast off

Cast off 2 sts, *sl remaining st on right-hand needle to left-hand needle, cast on 2 sts, cast off 4 sts*. Rep from * to * to end.

Making up

Sew in loose ends by weaving them into stitches at the back of your work. With right side facing, use a mattress stitch to join the side seams of the pattern component of the boot cuff. Sew up the rib on the rear side of the boot cuff.

These boot cuffs have the luxurious feel of alpaca. They are the perfect finishing touch for long, elegant boots.

Puss-in-Boots

Materials:

100g hank of textured aran yarn – mid-blue light

4 x large wooden buttons

Needles:

1 pair of 5.5mm (UK 5; US 9) single-pointed knitting needles

Large-eyed tapestry needle

Instructions:

Make two.

Using 5.5mm (UK 5; US 9) needles cast on 54 sts in mid-blue light yarn.

Row 2: Knit into the back of sts to form a neat edge.

Row 3: *k2, p2* rep to last 2 sts, k2.

Row 4: *p2, k2* rep to last 2 sts, p2.

Row 5: As row 4.

Row 6: As row 3.

Rows 7–24: Repeat rows 3–6 four more times and then rows 3 and 4 once more.

Row 25: Cast off 6sts then *k1, p1* to end of the row.

Rows 26–40: *p1, k1* rep.

Row 41: Cast off sts leaving a long piece of yarn to sew up seams.

Making up

With right side facing, use a mattress stitch to join the side seams of the rib component of the boot cuff. Turn the boot cuff inside out and sew the cast-off flap on to the main body of the cuff with a neat hemming stitch. Sew up the flap on the reverse side. Sew in loose strands of yarn.

Using your yarn, sew one button at the top edge of the flap and one at the bottom edge of the flap.

The blue wool and decorative wooden buttons look great with jeans and will fit any wide-topped boot. The colour can easily be changed to suit your wardrobe. The pattern is a double moss stitch and is suitable for a knitter who has mastered the basics.

Pig in the Grass

Materials:

100g hank of aran weight (50% Aran, 50% alpaca) yarn – dark green (A)

100g hank of aran yarn – light pink (B)

Needles:

1 pair of 5.5mm (UK 5; US 9) single-pointed knitting needles

1 pair of 5mm (UK 6; US 8) single-pointed knitting needles

Large-eyed tapestry needle

This is a bolder design of cuff, and it is especially suited to adding character to wellies or wide-legged boots.

36

Instructions:

Make two.

Using 5.5mm (UK 5; US 9) needles and cast on 58sts in A.

Row 2: Knit into the back of sts to form a neat edge.

Rows 3–4: st st.

Knitting note

Twist the yarn every three to four stitches to avoid long loops at the back of your work.

Pattern

Start reading the chart from the right-hand side.

Complete chart rows 1–20, starting with a knit row. Cut off yarn B. Change to size 5mm (UK 6; US 8) needles.

Ribbing

Row 1: *k2, p2* rep to last 2 sts, k2.

Row 2: *p2, k2* rep to last 2 sts, p2.

Rows 3–20: Rep rows 1 and 2.

Row 21: As row 1.

Row 22: Cast off sts leaving sufficient yarn to sew side seam.

Making up

Sew in loose ends by weaving them into stitches at the back of your work. With right side facing, use a mattress stitch to join the side seams of the pattern component of the boot cuff. Sew up the rib on the rear side of the boot cuff.

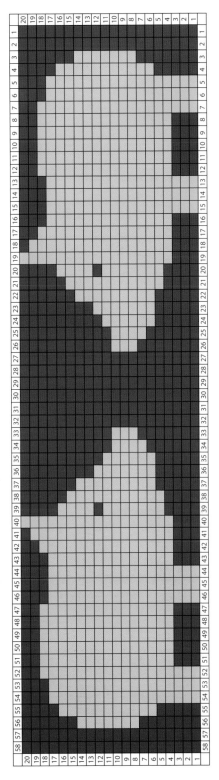

Sunrise

Materials:

100g hanks of aran weight (50% aran, 50% alpaca) yarn – black (A), orange (C) and red (D)

100g hank of textured aran weight yarn – green (B)

Needles:

1 pair of 5.5mm (UK 5; US 9) single-pointed knitting needles

Large-eyed tapestry needle

Instructions:

Make two.

Pattern

Cast on 54sts using yarn A. Knit into the back of the sts to form a neat edge. Cut off yarn A.

Start working from the chart working from right to left, repeating sts 1–27 once more to match the 54sts on your needle. Odd rows are knit and even rows are purl.

To make working with colour A easier, cut off four lengths of 100cm (39¼in) to twist it in at the appropriate points in the pattern.

At the end of row 15, cut off all colours except B, which will be used for the ribbing.

Ribbing

Using colour B, follow these instructions:

Row 1: *k3, p3* rep to end.

Rows 2–22: rep row 1.

Cast off sts, leaving sufficient yarn to sew up the side seam.

Making up

Sew in loose ends by weaving them into stitches at the back of your work.

With right side facing, use a mattress stitch to join the side seams of the pattern component of the boot cuff. Sew up the rib on the rear side of the boot cuff.

Knitting note

Twist the yarn every three to four sts to avoid long loops at the back of your work.

A	B	C	D

	27	26	25	24	23	22	21	20	19	18	17	16	15	14	13	12	11	10	9	8	7	6	5	4	3	2	1	
16																												16
15																												15
14																												14
13																												13
12																												12
11																												11
10																												10
9																												9
8																												8
7																												7
6																												6
5																												5
4																												4
3																												3
2																												2
1																												1
	27	26	25	24	23	22	21	20	19	18	17	16	15	14	13	12	11	10	9	8	7	6	5	4	3	2	1	

The inspiration for these bright boot cuffs came from colours I had seen on a delightful Art Deco vase. This pattern is suitable for a knitter with some experience due to the complexity of the pattern. The cuffs themselves are suitable for walking boots, short boots or long fashion boots.

Parisienne

Materials:

100g hanks of aran weight (50% Aran, 50% alpaca) yarn – walnut (A), black (B)

Needles:

1 pair of 5mm (UK 6; US 8) single-pointed knitting needles

1 pair of 4.5mm (UK 7; US 7) single-pointed knitting needles

Large-eyed tapestry needle

Instructions:

Make two.

Using 5mm (UK 6; US 8) needles, cast on 54sts in yarn A.

Rows 1–21: p1 *k3, p3* rep from * to * to end of row.

Row 22: As above, increasing 1 stitch in 27th stitch (55sts).

Pattern

Row 1: k7, *yo, sl1, k1, psso knit st, k2, k2tog, yo, k3*. Rep from * to * ending last repeat with k6.

Row 2 and all even numbered rows: purl

Row 3: k8, *yo, sl1, k1, psso, k2tog, yo, k5*. Rep from * to * ending last repeat with k7.

Row 5: k9, *yo, sl1, k1, psso, k7*. Rep from * to *, ending last repeat with k8.

Rows 6–17: Rep rows 1–6 twice more.

Cut off yarn A, leaving sufficient yarn to sew up your seam.

Row 18: Join in yarn B and knit to end.

Picot point cast off

Cast off 2 sts *slip remaining st on right-hand needle on to left-hand needle, cast on 2 sts using cable method, cast off 4sts*. Rep from * to * until you reach the end of the row. Fasten off last stitch.

Making up

Sew in loose ends by weaving them into stitches at the back of your work.

With right side facing, use a mattress stitch to join the side seams of the pattern component of the boot cuff.

Sew up the rib on the rear side of the boot cuff.

Bows

Make two.

Using 5mm (UK 6; US 8) needles, cast on 7sts in yarn A.

Row 1: p1, *k1, p1*. Rep from * to * twice more.

Repeat the above until work measures 8cm (1¼in). Sew in ends.

Take a length of yarn B and wind it round the centre of the strip to make your bow. Sew in ends and fasten the bow to the centre the front of the boot cuff.

These chic boot cuffs will fit snugly into the top of boots of any length. They combine a lace effect and a picot edge to add style, and are suitable for an experienced knitter.

Fair Isle

Materials:

100g hank of aran yarn – cream (A)

100g hank of aran weight (50% aran, 50% alpaca) yarn – blue (B)

50g hank of DK pure alpaca yarn – gold (C)

Needles:

1 pair of 5mm (UK 6; US 8) single-pointed knitting needles

Large-eyed tapestry needle

Instructions:

Make two.

Using 5mm (UK 6; US 8) needles, cast on 52sts in yarn A.

Row 2: k tbl.

Pattern

Row 1: *k1C, k3B*. Rep to the end of the row.

Row 2: p1C, p1B, *p3C, p1B*. Rep to last 2 sts, p2C.

Row 3: k2C, *k1B, k3C*. Rep to last 2 sts, k1B, k1C.

Row 4: *p3B, p1C *. Rep to the end of the row.

Row 5: Change to yarn A, knit to end.

Row 6: purl to end.

Rows 7–18: Repeat rows 1–6 twice more.

Rows 19–34: *k2, p2*. Rep * to * to end.

Row 35: Cast off sts.

Making up

Sew in loose ends by weaving them into stitches at the back of your work. With right side facing use a mattress stitch to join side seams of the pattern component of the boot cuff. Sew up rib on the rear side of the boot cuff.

These fantastic Fair Isle pattern boot cuffs will keep your feet cosy on a cold winter's day. They will suit walking boots very well.

Quackers

Materials:

50g hanks of DK pure alpaca yarn – teal (A), turquoise (B), gold (C), Chile red (D)

Needles:

1 pair of 5mm (UK 6; US 8) single-pointed knit

1 pair of 4.5mm (UK 7; US 7) single-pointed kr

Large-eyed tapestry needle

Instructions:

Make two.

Using 5mm (UK 6; US 8) needles, cast on 50sts in yarn A.

Row 1: k tbl to form a neat edge. Change to 4.5mm (UK 7; US 7) needles.

Rows 2–16: *k1, p1*. Cut off yarn A.

Pattern

Row 1: Using yarn B, knit row, increasing 1st in the middle (51st).

Row 2: purl.

Rows 3–13: Follow chart, working from right to left, and with the chart upside down (this is so the ducks are facing the right way when the boot cuff is completed).

Place motif on first row as follows: k4B, k4C, k9B, k4C, k9B, k4C, k9B, k4C, k4B. This is the set format for the pattern as the complete grid is repeated twice across the width of the boot cuff. All odd numbered rows are knit and even numbered rows are purl. Cut off yarn C.

Rows 14–16: st st.

Row 17: Cast off using picot cast off as follows: cast off 2 sts *slip remaining st on right-hand needle on to left-hand needle, cast on 2 sts using cable method, cast off 4sts*.

Rep from * to * until you reach the end of the row. Fasten off last stitch.

Making up

Sew in loose ends by weaving them into stitches at the back of your work. With right side facing, use a mattress stitch to join the side seams of the pattern component of the boot cuff. Sew up the rib on the rear side of the boot cuff.

> **Knitting note**
>
> Twist the yarn every three to four sts to avoid long loops at the back of your work.

B	C	D

	23	22	21	20	19	18	17	16	15	14	13	12	11	10	9	8	7	6	5	4	3	2	1	
12																								12
11																								11
10									■	■				■										10
9									■	■	■			■										9
8																								8
7																								7
6																								6
5																								5
4																								4
3																								3
2																								2
1																								1
	23	22	21	20	19	18	17	16	15	14	13	12	11	10	9	8	7	6	5	4	3	2	1	

Lovely weather for ducks! These boot cuffs look great and add character to children's wellies or boots. This pattern is suitable for a knitter who has mastered the basics.

Hearthlight

Materials:

100g hanks of Aran weight
(50% Aran, 50% alpaca) yarn
– sunset (A), mid blue (B)
and orange (C)

Needles:

1 pair of 4.5mm (UK 7; US 7) single-pointed knitting needles

1 pair of 5mm (UK 6; US 8) single-pointed knitting needles

Large-eyed tapestry needle

Instructions:

Make two.

Using 4.5mm (UK 7; US 7) needles,
cast on 52sts in yarn A.

Row 1: *k3, p3* rep to last 4sts, k3, 1.

Rows 2–16: Rep row 1.

Change to 5mm (UK 6; US 8) needles.

Pattern

Row 1: *k6B, k3A, k3B, k3A*, rep from * to *
twice more to last 7 sts, k6B, k1A.

Row 2: p1A, *p6b, p3A, p3B, p3A*. Rep from *
to * to last 6 sts, p6B.

Rows 3–8: Rep rows 1 and 2, three more times.

Row 9: *k6A, k3C, k3A, k3C*. Rep to last 7 sts,
k6A, k1C.

Row 10: p1C, *p6A, p3C, p3A, p3C*. Rep to last
6 sts, p6A.

Rows 11–12: Rep rows 1 and 2.

Rows 13–14: Rep rows 9 and 10. Cut off yarns
A and C.

Row 15: knit row in yarn B. Cast off sts in yarn B.

Making up

Sew in loose ends by weaving them into
stitches at the back of your work. With right
side facing, use a mattress stitch to join the
side seams of the pattern component of
the boot cuff. Sew up the rib on the rear
side of the boot cuff.

This is another design inspired by my love of Art Deco, and the bright colours are sure to cheer you up on a cold winter's day. These boot cuffs are suitable for walking boots, short boots or long fashion boots, and the pattern is suitable for a knitter with some experience.

Acknowledgements

Thanks to Jenny at Artesano Yarns for supplying all the yarns for the 20 projects and for her constant encouragement. Also to Kate at The Oak Studios for workspace and advice; and Niloufer for supplying tea and chocolate.

You are invited to visit the author's website: www.theknitknacks.co.uk

Publishers' Note

If you would like more information on knitting techniques, try:
Beginner's Guide to Knitting by Alison Dupernex, Search Press, 2004;
Twenty to Make: Knitted Beanies by Susie Johns, Search Press, 2012